It's Not Personal

Nigel Pantling

smith|doorstop

Published 2020 by
Smith|Doorstop Books
The Poetry Business
Campo House
54 Campo Lane
Sheffield S1 2EG

www.poetrybusiness.co.uk

ISBN 978-1-912196-35-7
Nigel Pantling hereby asserts his moral right to be
identified as the author of this book.

British Library Cataloguing-in-Publication Data.
A catalogue record for this book is available from the
British Library.

Design & typeset by Tim Morris
Printed and bound by CPI Group (UK) Ltd, Croydon, CR0 4YY

Smith|Doorstop Books is a member of Inpress:
www.inpressbooks.co.uk. Distributed by
NBN International, 1 Deltic Avenue,
Rooksley, Milton Keynes MK13 8LD.

The Poetry Business gratefully acknowledges the support
of Arts Council England.

Supported by
ARTS COUNCIL
ENGLAND

Contents

9   Something My Girlfriend Said to Me

10   First Times

11   Love Letter from My Pastry Cook

12   Crosswords

13   Visiting Sloane Square

14   Differences

15   Bath

16   After the Dream

17   Unlike Us

18   Cuba

19   Icebergs

20   Cleaning the Slate

22   According to *Every Woman's Doctor*

23   On Being Named After a Film Star

24   Battle of Britain

25   American Hard Gums

26   Moon-landing

27   Moving School

28   On the Way Home from Choir Practice

29   After Evensong

30   Tineke's Party

31   Death in the Family

     I   *Night*

     II   *Morning*

     III   *Funeral*

     IV   *Afterwards*

     V   *Transportation Theory*

36   Dog

37   Encounter

38   Lunch with the MI6 Recruiter

39   Final Interview for MI6

40   Signing the Act

41   I'm Googling My Name

42   Most Important Client

43   It's Business

44   Operational Risk

45   Armageddon in the Property Market

46   Consequences

49   The Answer

50   Evensong: Organist

51   Evensong: Verger

52   Evensong: Vicar

53   Evensong: Treble

54   Evensong: Bass

55   Evensong: Sidesman

56   The Battle of Arras

57   Lockerbie

58   Sandhurst Drill

59   Sandhurst Bull

60   Sandhurst Shouting

61   Sandhurst Uniform

63   Finding the House

64   Delivery

65   Distinctions

66   Slipping

67   T Shirts

68   My Mother Mistakes Her Phone for a Shoe

69   Alternative Spaces

70   Some Things about Last Christmas I'm Sure of

71   Loveshack

72   My Father Mows the Lawn

73   Seedling

For my sisters

Something My Girlfriend Said to Me

Do you remember, when you were a boy,
how the chimes of an ice-cream van
could bring on a rush of excitement,
how you struggled with the choice –
a strawberry mivvi, a rocket lolly,
or a 99 with hundreds and thousands –
how different each felt
in your mouth,
on your tongue,
how wonderful
it was to know that
if you chose a mivvi today,
you could still have a 99 tomorrow?
Well that's how it is with me and men.

First Times

After the first time, she said to him
'The first time is always awful,
isn't it?'

It was his first first time, in his first year,
in her shared room emptied of her room-mate
used to being asked to work in the library.

After that, his first times came and went,
in houses and halls, colleges and rooms,
home and away, indoors and outside,

baroque, bizarre, boring, bloody, bad,
but he would never say
they were awful.

Love Letter from My Pastry Cook

I want you to think of my heart as this egg.
Take it in your hand, fresh from its box –
how pale and undistinguished it appears.
Notice how inert it is: still, dry, silent.
Against your tongue it has no flavour,
smell it – there is nothing beyond a hint of earth,
in your palm it lacks the heft even of a pebble.

You know if you squeezed now
you could crush this egg of mine,
so treat it with care, keep it safely by you
ready for the moment:
                                take the trouble then
to open it gently, and what pleasure it will bring –
all the soufflés, cakes, and pastries you desire,
and, I promise, a chocolate mousse to die for.

Crosswords

She relished solving a crossword with her lovers,
folding herself round the current man in her bed
to measure his intellect against her own.

She gave each lover a cryptic crossword to himself:
Telegraph, Times, Guardian, Spectator, LRB
until there had been more paramours than puzzles.

Then she began to add rules of her own.
With J they did the across clues first.
K had to work up from the bottom right corner.

L must answer odd numbered clues before evens.
M just the ones where they already had a letter.
She switched to the General Knowledge Crossword

for N. Plumping the pillows and twining their legs,
she said they should only try clues with seven words
and with a transitive verb in the present tense.

'Fuck that,' he said, 'that's not what I came here to do.'

Visiting Sloane Square

Slithering down her stairs, his heels
    slam, slat by slat by slat, slashing
        his slight chance of slinking
            silently away. He's left a slick

where he slathered and slobbered
    on the sleek silk of her pillow-slip
        then slumped into the slotted
            slab of her Peter Jones bed.

He's praying she's still asleep as he slips the latch,
sliding into his Docs for the schlep up Sloane Street,
where the sleet is slapping slantwise against the slates.

Differences

In some parallel world,
where Fermat's Last Theorem has yet to be proven
and the rainbow has eleven colours,
they still had lunch together in Olivo's,
still laughed, flirted, drank too much wine,
leant forward on their chairs, elbows resting on linen.

And in that world, where there is no salt in the sea or the soup
and winter-flowering broccoli is orange,
he didn't move his hand those last six inches
to the freckled invitation of her forearm.

No, in that world where the alphabet runs from W to F
and the sun sets in the north and rises in the south
they drained their glasses, looked at their watches,
said gosh that was fun we must do it again,
and he is still married and has forgotten her name.

Bath

You're lying in the long tub you bought
when you first renovated the house,
before the children, so you could both fit in,
the water's hot and you've used the rose-scented bubble bath
so you're half-covered in foam
and through the squares of yellow and pink glass
you put in the top frame of the window
you can see the clouds pass looking just like the foam,
and life is good
because you're 35, there's Bach on the radio,
and you're thinking about the au pair
whose skirt rides up when she's driving
and you're in the passenger seat.

When your wife comes in, she sits on the window-seat,
her mouth smiles and she says,
'You do know that I'm seeing someone else?'
and when you say 'It's not Robert is it?'
because that would be too close to home
she says 'no it's Jack' and you say 'do you love him?'
and then you get out of the bath and dress
and you both go downstairs to the garden
where the children are playing in the sand pit
and you open a bottle of the good Chablis.

After the Dream

Waking was hard, as if
dragging himself up from the deep
against the pull of where he'd been,
and when at last his head broke clear
it was not to brightness or new horizons
or to thoughts of escape or relief
but simply to the release of breath

breath that for too long had been held close
was suddenly plentiful and free
so free, he soon forgot that breathing
was anything at all and before long
all that was left of that dark time
was the feeling that something,
somewhere, was not quite right.

Unlike Us

The Spanish, he'd once told her,
have a word for sensitivity to cold.
She remembers this later, when
his touch swerves from her skin,
their conversation loses fine detail
and he takes to leaving the room
whenever she comes in. At night
as they lie apart she breathes
friolera friolera friolera friolera.

Cuba

Walking back to our cabin in Playa La Boca
listening to salsa seeping through shutters
to the backbeat of the sea
talking about our supper
at the paladar of Señora Lopez
about her cooking and her kindness
how she'd gone outside to leave us
to enjoy our *ropa vieja* in her only living room,
we were looking forward to making love by moonlight
with the windows open to the breeze and all seemed right and true and good,
so even the sight of a spider the size of a dinner plate by our cabin door
couldn't change our mood,
                              and though we didn't know what was being said
back home and everything it would lead to, if we had I'm sure
we'd still have swayed to the jazz,
still eaten all the steak and rice, still reached out in the half-dark.

Icebergs

The cocktail bar is on the foredeck,
square tables with diagonal cloths,
glass bowls of cashews and olives.

He orders a Manhattan on the rocks, tells himself
not to joke to the waiter about the Titanic,
and settles for the round trip to Hampton Court,

lunch, with no stopping: perfect for tourists,
lovers and divorced men with nothing
better to do on a summer afternoon.

London sidles past on either bank: the Eye,
House of Lords, Lambeth Palace, the Tate.
He's draining the last of his second drink,

when there she is at the bar with someone,
sparkling in conversation. He realises
how little they'd talked, how much stayed hidden.

Cleaning the Slate

2019

Only *beloved* showing through the mat
of couch grass and wild strawberry.
I kneel, push my hand through the green
feeling the harshness of sand and salt.
I'll wash and scour the slate
before I polish, before I can make good.

2014

Harvest festival at St Minver's today.
I go to the vestry for water and find
pyramids of paw-paws, pineapples,
mangoes, as if the congregation
has salvaged the cargo
of a wrecked East Indiaman.

2011

In those last hours,
we filled the gaps
when you would have answered.
Everyone up-beat,
in case you were listening
and reading between the silences.

2009

Tourists parking, taking ferries
for slots, shopping, fish and chips;
laughter wavers on the wind, sunlight
glancing off the Pride of Padstow
pierces the stained glass.

2007

I've forgotten secateurs,
so I pull and twist at the grass
thinking of the night nurses
levering you from bed
for five pointless steps: don't they
teach them to see death coming?

2006

Bleak flat winter.
Shadow of stone
across cut turf.
Your neat slate
just proud.

According to Every Woman's Doctor

        conception can take place
up to three days after intercourse.
So it was that I was conceived,
not long after the war,
on the upper deck of a Number 38 bus
between Crouch End and Muswell Hill.

Tired from scouring the shops,
my mother leant back on the tartan
gripping the seat corner against the jolts.
She carried bacon, bread, butter and eggs,
one of which, she would soon find,
had been fertilised.

On Being Named After a Film Star

Every Saturday evening while she was pregnant,
my mother went to see Nigel Patrick at the Odeon.

She nibbled popcorn as he overcame impossible odds,
leading a platoon of soldiers against the Desert Fox,

nursing his Lancaster home on one arthritic engine,
or captaining a Corvette across the capricious ocean.

She must have hoped all this would rub off on me
by some cinematic Law of Nominative Determinism.

When, years later, he switched to playing the villain
she took to watching me out of the corner of her eye.

Battle of Britain

The home-time bell: we scramble
lining up in our V on the grass,
Able, Baker, Charlie, Dog ...
September sun low in our eyes
we carry out pre-flight checks:
penknife, skewer, string;
Beano, Dandy, Eagle;
sherbet, black-jacks, gum;
matches, Roger? Fags?
Thumbs up all round.
We're ready for take-off.

American Hard Gums

It's Wednesday evening,
Journey Into Space on the radio,
broadcast just for Mum and me.

The gas fire is chuntering
as it warms our knees on the rug.
The spacecraft's air-lock hisses,

but I keep one ear cocked
for the rustle of the sweet-bag,
hoping there's time for one more,
one more before the music comes.

Moon-landing

We had sausages for supper that evening,
on trays in front of the TV,
making an exception to Mum's rule.
She brought the food through
just as he came down the ladder

so I missed the actual moment
when his foot hit the ground.
I heard his voice, though, talking about steps
as if he were reading the football results:
United States of America, one, Russia, nil.

Later, halfway through the apple crumble,
the flag went up, held out sideways by wire,
looking as if there was a good strong wind.
And after I went to bed he hit a golf ball,
apparently, but no-one knows where it went.

Moving School

He doesn't know why they came to this damp house
with its weedy garden over-run by snapping dogs.
Or why he had to leave his old school for this one,
a bus ride away, a bus which never has a seat for him.

He doesn't know what they're saying in the playground
with their funny way of talking, words that to him
mean nothing, so when he stares he gets another kick.
But he does know his clothes are wrong. Too new,

like the grey blazer his mother says he must take care of
because there won't be another for a very long time,
or too old, like the grey shorts that came second-hand.
Everything is grey in this school. Even the angry faces.

He walks alone from the bus stop, across the no-man's-land,
stopping beside one of the clay pools, loaded with old doors
and used tyres, scummy with slime and oil. He makes a pile
of his school clothes, the precious blazer folded on top

and slides feet first into the strange water, all the way in,
rolling over until from toes to hair he is coated in grey.

On the Way Home from Choir Practice

He was older and bigger than me, and his punch
was as glorious and unexpected as
when we trebles hit the top A in the Kyrie.
I'd done nothing to deserve that.
Oh my outrage as I named him to the police.
I wanted him tracked down, humiliated, punished.

The doubts took years. Had I provoked him?
Maybe I'd exaggerated my shock and the pain?
His mother, when she came round to apologise,
blaming it all on her being so ill with the cancer:
how had she deserved that? And how had he?
I'd pressed charges: where was the mercy in that?

After Evensong

After I've hung my cassock
and surplice in the vestry,

once I've helped to count
the collection and gather

the hymn books, and while
'At Even, Ere the Sun Was Set'

is still setting my feet tapping,
you drive us to the Greyhound.

The sign says "Sunday night, eight o'clock,
Miss Iris Towl at the piano".

I sit in the pub garden with the Smiths crisps
and lemonade you bring out, and I worry about

the strange turbaned floweriness of this pianist,
whose music might charm you and carry you off

but the melodies that shimmy through the window
are by Cole Porter. It's me they enslave.

Tineke's Party

Remember that time at Tineke's, John?
You were part of her crowd by then,
talked their slang, shared their crazes,
knew the best bands, the right records.

I was there because I lived nearby.
She and I would walk the fifty yards
from the bus stop, my satchel bumping
against her hip, my tongue locked.

"Dress brightly" the invitation said,
written on a card from WH Smith.
You went in purple flares and tie-dye.
I wore a V-neck and my sports jacket.

Everyone who mattered was there:
Simon, who'd already had sex twice,
cocky Micky, obviously a chancer,
Roger, who promised to roll a reefer

but never did. Someone took a photo –
twelve of us, posed and awkward.
I'm at the front, playing air guitar.
Tineke's at one side, looking at you.

Death in the Family

I   Night

That night
she set the body in a shoe box
waiting for a coffin small enough.

That night
she baulked at telling the boy
fearful he would not cope.

That night
she spent upstairs alone.
Silent.

That night
she started down the road
that would take her away.

The boy slept well that night,
dreaming of riding his bike
with his new sister.

II   *Morning*

The house is dull
his mother nowhere to be seen
his father grey as ash.

A muffled phone call
he catches only the words
'not been baptised'.

Later he takes a note to school
they let him sit at the back
colouring in.

III   Funeral

His father borrowed fifty pounds
from a colleague at Nestlé.
It didn't stretch to a headstone.

On the day itself they kept him away,
and since then no-one has taken him back
to let him mark the place.

Now only his parents know.
When they go, they will take his chance
to find her and say

Oh my Sister, what fun we would have had.

IV   *Afterwards*

Afterwards,
his mother had only miscarriages.
Wrung out with the pain of it all
she found herself locked away
in a hospital miles from home.
He wonders now how that felt,
to lose the living as well as the dead.

V   *Transportation Theory*

He finds it easy, this mathematical algorithm
for minimising the distance travelled
when visiting a fixed number of scattered points.
He answers the question and thinks of his father,
little older than him and a sales rep for Nestlé,
parked in some lay-by on the North York Moors
scouring the map for the shortest route
to the day's quota of village sweetshops
and small town grocers distrustful of southerners
and preferring to stick with Rowntree thank you very much,
and his father not able to solve the problem
and fearful of returning too early or too late
to the dull house and the wrung-out wife
and still bringing no money for the headstone
while around him the rain layers off the moor.

Dog

(Poem almost using a line by C K Williams)

When I find him again it's two o'clock in the morning in my grim hotel on the
    central square

and he's not as I remembered – smaller, shaggier and with no teeth on one side –
    but still

unquestionably the same dog, and as I reach my hand to ruffle his coat he looks
    at me shiftily,

like one who has been starved of affection, his moments measured in curses, kicks
    and well-aimed stones;

and now having insinuated himself into this grimy hotel bar he sits, looking for all
    the world

like a commercial traveller, booked in late to find reception empty and obliged to
    wait

brooding on the many petty injustices of the day, while still trusting that a kind
    providence

will bring the key to a warm room and a clean bed, or in his case, a share of an
    overlooked digestive biscuit.

Encounter

Are all teas the same? she asks,
from her seat across the aisle
disturbing my Metro reading
on an early District Line train.
She holds up a card, the letter T
printed in stylised black on grey.

Are some Ts similar but not the same
and what does it mean to be similar?
Is quite similar the same as similar,
and how can things be a bit similar?
And can books be similar to boxes,
and can two rocks be the same?

The sweat wells on my back.
I force my eyes to stay on hers.
In the black glass behind
I see a middle-aged couple
in philosophical conversation
about the meaning of 'like'.

It's just that I'm not sure how much
it matters that all Ts are the same.

Lunch with the MI6 Recruiter

We've successfully navigated our introductory lunch –
me, my wife, the recruiter, his wife –
in the Castelreagh Room at the Foreign and Military Club:
prawn cocktail, steak and kidney pud, a decent claret
(apparently) and now we're in the drawing room for coffee,
easy chairs at an oblong table, him and me side by side,
our wives sitting opposite, his wife facing him,
and he's just telling me about life as an MI6 officer
based in an embassy abroad, about your cover
as a cultural attaché or some other nondescript job,
when I notice his wife looking over his shoulder
at Members coming for coffee and liable to overhear,
and when they're looming up she taps on the table
with a red-nailed fingertip, one tap for each loomer.

You have to understand my boy, he says, your status
in a foreign embassy will always be low *Tap Tap*
I fear the Aussies will have a field day at The Oval
next week it means your wife will have to get used
to being married to an apparently unsuccessful diplomat
Tap Boycott's your man to take the pace off the ball
of course and not mixing as an equal *Tap Tap* did you
see his century at Lord's with the senior men of the Office
can be dispiriting but your pay was a handy opening bat
at school and rations are properly taken care of and an
off spinner too I took seven for fifty four and if you're
good at your job in a match against Stonyhurst there'll be
back in fifty eight a knighthood for you at the end of it
Tap Tap Tap Tap would you care for a cigar?

Final Interview for MI6

I

There are five of them this time, seated in a row.
No introductions and no name cards.
They give you a hard time but you keep going.

Then the young woman, surely the most junior
but doing most of the talking, tells you to imagine
you're in a hostile country, and to choose one of them
to be the local you have to entrap, suborn, entice,
seduce or otherwise persuade to come over.

She gives that look you've got wrong before, so you choose
the blimp beside her, and greeting him like an old friend,
commiserate on his child's poor health, and then pretend
you've had him photographed as he takes your gift of cash.

When you arrive home, the offer letter is on the doormat.

II

Slippery bastard chose me. 'Hello Mikhail, it's good to see you,
let's have a beer, and I'm so sorry to hear the baby's poorly'.
Chummy as you like. Perfectly believable. Of course I just blinked.
Took some time to get to the point, but at last he offered me cash,
for "medical treatment", one diplomat to another, no questions asked.
When he mentioned the camera, it could have been me thirty years ago.
I was for saying no. But none of the others had been in the field.

Signing the Act

Sign here, he says, passing across a blank sheet of paper,
to confirm you understand your obligation to the Office,
and won't talk about what you do while working here,
no matter how minor you suppose your role. Remember:
the smallest detail may have a significance you cannot imagine.

Here is the list of fifty-seven countries you cannot visit
in case you give comfort to Her Majesty's enemies
or are tempted into compromise or indiscretion.
You will notice that Arcadia and Utopia are included:
the Secretary of State wishes the list to be future-proof.

Just my little joke.
No, we cannot allow you to take a copy.
Nor may you write down any of the wording.
Even to refer to this document or to our meeting
constitutes a breach of the Official Secrets Act.

I'm Googling My Name

as you do when you're supposed to be working, and there among references
to the address of my business, my letter to *The Independent* ten years ago,
and to the Nigel Pantling who's a primary school teacher in Sandgate,
I see a link to the Thatcher archives.
                                        I click through and I'm deep in
the Miners' Strike, and someone with my name has written a speech for the
Prime Minister in praise of the police. OK, well that won't be me then,
Labour voter, Yorkshire kid, culturally suspicious of the plods, more likely
to be out on the picket lines, standing shoulder to shoulder.
                                                            I check the date.
Wait, though, I was at the Home Office then, and I did write speeches.
But that can't be my language, my tone, my rhetoric: that speech
doesn't stack up with me as a socially responsible principled young man.

Ah, but there it is. I was young then, and ambitious, diligent, eager to please:
all things that have led principled men to lie for their country.

Most Important Client

It's 8.59, and time for my daily call to my Most Important Client.

I dial: Good Morning Michael, I say.

Don't tell me it's a good morning, he says,

If I want to know if it's a good morning I'll ask you.

Now why is our fucking share price down 20p today?

I don't know, I say.

Then fucking well find out, he says.

I ring the stockbroker, another Michael.

Morning Michael, I say, I've just been speaking to our mutually

Most Important Client, and he wonders why his share price is down 20p today?

I don't know he says, perhaps there are more Sellers than Buyers?

Ah, I say, will you ring Michael and tell him that?

No fucking fear, he says, that's your job.

It's Business

she said, from the chair
he still thought of as his.
New owners, new outlook:
we need to make changes,
show we're serious, starting
at the top. Nothing personal.

Nothing personal, not to do
with your management style,
the quality of your team,
your rapport with suppliers,
or relationships with clients:
all good. No, it's business.

Just business: we're pleased
with margins and cash flow,
so we'll pay half your bonus
and your long-term incentive.
It's just that I'm taking over.
Like I said, it's not personal.

Operational Risk

It's not like credit risk, market risk or liquidity risk,
it's not a permissive risk, where you can say, OK,
we will take an acceptable level of exposure,
in pursuit of a quantifiable reward.
No, it's a different risk, it's related to inherent factors,
factors you can't control, measure or predict,
like the risk a systems programmer misses a key stroke
and cocks-up the coding of your Black-Scholes model,
or someone doesn't do the Know Your Counter-Party checks,
or an invisible glitch in your website turns away customers,
or like the time your most trusted employee
met the competition in a Morrison's car park
and handed over confidential information
for a brown paper bag of fifty pound notes.

Armageddon in the Property Market
(with thanks to the glossary provided by Quintain Estates and Development PLC)

Is when passing rent equals interest if no tenants renew and all breaks are exercised
where passing rent is the contracted rent receivable annually from the property
or if that property is a mixed use development, with retail as well as offices
then its gross development value is current market value when complete
provided there is resolution to grant (subject to section 106 agreement
between the authority) so the total return defined as the movement
in net asset value per share adjusted by percentage and dividend
will be compared to interest cover which is pre-tax profits
before interest divided, causing average gearing
or the ratio of net borrowings given
less cash to shareholders.

Consequences

Tuesday eleven o'clock

Something's happened
somewhere a mistake
some misjudgement
the press are on to it.

Down here she's busy
with damage limitation
preparing a statement
reassuring her clients.

The fear from upstairs
is staining the ceiling.

Tuesday one o'clock

Loyalty has to be a two-way thing,
she'd told him at final interview.
People like me go the extra mile
if they know you'll support them.

He'd smiled across the table then,
now he's questioning her judgement
she can tell by the tone of his voice
he's forgotten that conversation.

Out of my hands, he says, no choice –
confidential inquiry by outside lawyers
reporting to the Board – no suggestion you
personally have done anything wrong.

Now I need you to hand over your phone:
your secretary has given me your diary,
your papers and access to your computer.
Of course, you continue to have our support.

A week later

You want to see our terms of reference?
We're sure you'll understand
we're not here to answer your questions
and the secret nature of our inquiry
prevents us revealing why we're asking.
All will be clear from the direction of travel.

Tell us: did you take all due steps to assess risk
with a view to preventing this egregious error?
If not, we shall deduce you were negligent
for failing to anticipate this outcome.
If so, we shall decide you chose to proceed
in the face of a clear and present threat.

Now tell us about your management of juniors.
Did you know what they were doing?
If so, we shall conclude you colluded with them.
If not, we shall find your supervision inadequate.
And what of your seniors: is it acceptable to you
that they were unaware of what was going on?

There are other things that concern us,
which we feel no need to ask you about.
We shall rely on evidence from third parties,
including those you worked for
and the staff who worked for you.
Now do you have any questions?

No, we cannot state the accusations against you,
or comment on the timing of our inquiry,
or say who we are talking to or why.
And our conclusions will inevitably be bound
by an onerous burden of confidentiality.
But is there anything else we can assist you with?

A month later

Her boss calls her to an unscheduled meeting.
She finds the Head of HR is with him.
On the desk between them a thick report,
tricked out with a dozen coloured flags.

They do not give her a copy of the report.
They do not show her the flagged pages.
Instead they take it in turns
to read to her selected sentences.

They do not invite comment or response.
They tell her to hand over her security pass
on her way out of the building.
She looks away, up at the white ceiling.

The Answer

After two hours, my screen's full
of well-expressed emptiness:
my record of the clever answer
I gave yesterday in conversation
with a client in a sharp suit
who had an even sharper problem
he expected me to solve.

Today, I'm meeting my obligation
to put the answer down on paper,
and I have to give the answer
such order, structure and clarity
that it will be pleasing to him,
and I must also express the answer
in terms that mean he cannot sue me
if with the benefit of his hindsight
the answer turns out to be wrong.

I return to this struggle.
This is when I remember
why it is I hate writing things down
and why the answer is always just to talk.

Evensong: Organist

Stanley Claymore, whose organ playing in a diocesan concert
was indistinguishable from the mighty Wurlitzer, according to
his best friend who'd been sitting at the back of the nave,
is working his way enthusiastically through some Palestrina.

He's choirmaster too, and against the odds in a small town
he's built a strong complement of male voices, even an alto.
As he accompanies the hymns he keeps an eye on his son,
there among the trebles, his hope for the future of the choir.

One day, the adult son will carry the organist's coffin
and learning from that experience become an undertaker,
burying over the years the parents of his fellow trebles,
and most of the basses and tenors who'd sung for his father.

Evensong: Verger

Too young for the first war, too old for the second,
he'd circled the globe in the Merchant Navy.
Now he steers the double file of choristers
from vestry door to the step of the sanctuary
where they peel off alternately into their stalls
like incendiary shells from a Roman candle.

Never one to stay for the evening service,
he slips sideways through the Lady Chapel
and home to his tied cottage, to brew tea,
check the pools with the *Sunday Sketch*,
and read with disbelief about John Glenn
orbiting Earth three times in three hours.

Evensong: Vicar

The Reverend Edmund, more subdued in black and white and plain tippet
than in the green cope and the biretta of the morning's Eucharist
counts a congregation of twenty, adequate for an undistinguished Sunday,
the Twenty Second after Trinity, and a rainy autumn evening.

This has been an easy parish, and while he's still unhappy
at the long hair and lack of discipline of some of the Youth Group,
at least he's avoided the problems of those of his contemporaries
faced with modernisers on their Parochial Church Councils

wanting everyday language in the liturgy and skiffle in the nave.
True, when he came here Evensong brought in sixty or more
but these days congregations are falling everywhere aren't they?
He's sure he can look forward to a more desirable living next.

Evensong: Treble

At five to six he lights the sanctuary candles
with a wick threaded through a brass snuffer,
checking over his shoulder for girls to impress
and to see if his parents are ready in their seats,
three pews back on the Gospel side, or yet again
arriving late halfway through the introit hymn.

A red band and brass medallion, set off nicely
by the white of his surplice, tell his seniority.
Beneath his cassock his clothes are muddied
from a churchyard game of British Bulldog;
in his pocket, ready for the sermon, the latest
Commando with an exciting story of violence.

Evensong: Bass

The Tallow brothers know their role is always to be here,
underpinning the choir, their deep tone steadying
a congregation uncertain about rhythm and pitch.

Sidney, a snowy sparrow, is eight years older than tall Walter:
they've clocked up a combined century of solid bass line,
with none of the showy unreliability of the altos and tenors.

Their brother Frank used to stand between them in the stalls
until one Wartime Sunday the vicar forgot to honour
Frank's eldest son, killed in action. He left the choir that night

and never returned. Sidney and Walter keep the gap open,
declining to shuffle closer, even when space is short
on summer evenings when the basses turn out in force.

Evensong: Sidesman

He's done this for forty years. Now he's eighty
and greeting the handful of regulars, handing out
hymn books and psalters, and taking them in again
is so much better than sitting at home on his own.

But finishing at seven fifteen is early when you've nothing
to go back to. Counting the collection, switching out lights
and checking that doors are locked takes longer each year
than can be accounted for by the natural slowing of age.

Afterwards, passing the bright windows on Church Road,
he imagines the choir, home for sandwiches in front of the TV –
Sunday Night at the London Palladium, with *Beat the Clock*
and Bruce Forsyth asking 'Can you come back next week?'

The Battle of Arras

i.m. Horace Pantling, died 28th April 1917

Foresters have been in this oak wood.
Around me lie the ruins of giants,
thick trunks quartered and split,
sap oozing where boughs were lopped,
foliage fallen in tangled heaps –
impossible to say what belongs to what –
the crispness and brightness leached away:
the only trees still standing
spared by a spot of blue paint.
I think of Arras, and my great uncle –
a countryman before he volunteered –
walking tall uphill towards the ridgeline,
hearing bullets pass like buzz saws,
and wondering if he carries a blue mark.

Lockerbie

i.m. Timothy Burman, died 21st December 1988

A likeable young man, a recent recruit
in a hurry to prove himself,
putting his hand to every task
on call to work for any Director
sure to volunteer for every pitch
getting the knack of the new computer
first to his desk and last from the office
never seeing his home in daylight.

A very likeable man, tidying his desk,
ticking off tasks from his pencilled list:
merger schedules passed to team leader;
dividend analysis completed and sent;
briefing done for Directors' meeting;
posting yellow notes for colleagues
updating, cajoling, reminding them
they're covering for him over Christmas.

Such a likeable man, off to New York,
pulling his suitcase from under his desk
deflecting the barbs of envious team mates
shouldering his coat as he runs to the lift
down and down and out onto Cheapside
ignoring the amber signs on taxis
taking a tube as the safest way
to check-in on time for seat 34G.

Sandhurst Drill

Foot drill: the graduate entry officers are on the Square
Quick March   About Turn   Mark Time
sweating into their combat kit, anxious to escape the eye
of the Grenadier Guards drill sergeant standing stock still
Right Turn   Left Turn   Change Step
pressed and polished to perfection, cap peak
jutting over his forehead like the beak of a bird of prey
Parade Halt   Slope Arms   Stand at Ease.

One of them has not escaped. Second Lieutenant Claber,
commissioned from Cambridge into the Education Corps,
has been marching with his left arm and leg forward together,
then, inevitably, with his right arm and leg doing the same.
Come along, Mister Claber, Sir, you're supposed to be an intelligent gentleman.
What did they teach you at university? You look like fucking Spotty-Dog.

Sandhurst Bull

Eleven at night, 'Hey Jude' on the record player.

I'm bulling my drill boots, rubbing spit and black polish
into the leather, its dimples flattened yesterday
by repeated application of the back of a hot spoon
according to the traditional Sandhurst technique.

The piano slides from F to C to B flat until the coda
flips C for E flat and spins on and on and on and on

and under my fingers the Cherry Blossom swirls and swirls
like grooves on vinyl and after seven minutes eleven seconds
I lift the needle back to the start. At two, I'll leave the boots
and begin to bull my Sam Browne with dark tan

and 'Here Comes the Sun'.

Sandhurst Shouting

Nothing he's achieved is as good as this.
Nothing at school or university, no sport,

no challenge he's ever taken on.
He, with a fear of heights so great

he can't look over a cinema balcony,
has climbed the Sandhurst scaffolding tower –

eighty feet of vertical poles with no safety net –
and reaching the parallel bars at the very top

has stood upright and shuffled along, his rifle held
above his head, fresh air between him and ground.

This matters. And all it has taken
is personal abuse from a staff sergeant
and not wanting to let the others down.

Sandhurst Uniform

A staff sergeant meets them from the train:
he tells them on this first day at Sandhurst
to accept all the shouting, the drill and bull
– the burnishing of their boots and uniform –
it's what they have to do if they're to pass:
and soon they'll go home on weekend leave.

But they won't go home on weekend leave:
it's part of the staff sergeant's plan to train
the cadets to accept that months must pass
before they'll get away from Sandhurst.
To keep them here, he'll say their uniform
is too untidy or their boots need more bull.

If the staff sergeant says he wants more bull,
then more bull there will have to be, to leave
glinting boots and knife-creased uniform,
with double spit and polish. The cadets train
to switch off their minds: while at Sandhurst
they operate on automatic to let weeks pass.

When the staff sergeant gives a two-day pass
they go home to tell their girlfriends that bull
is essential to their education, that Sandhurst
has it just right, that no-one wants to leave
out a single thing the Army is doing to train
them to be fit to wear Her Majesty's uniform.

Reporting back, as they put on their uniform
the staff sergeant says that if they're to pass
at the Sovereign's Parade they'll have to train
to the highest standards yet. Still more bull
and more drill, yet no-one wants to leave,
nor even thinks of giving up on Sandhurst.

It's not an option to give up on Sandhurst:
they're all determined to wear this uniform
as commissioned officers when they leave.
They have to stay the course, they must pass:
for that they accept the shouting, the bull,
the numbing monotony it brings in its train.

After the Parade they leave together for the train,
and everyone has passed. They came to Sandhurst
individuals: drill, bull, shouting made them uniform.

Finding the House

I'd stopped for a pee at a dog-leg in a lane, by a patch of hard-standing
where a farmer piled pig-shit, and the steam was rising through the snow
slanting in the north easterly which stunts the trees in that part of Suffolk.

As I zipped up and brushed snow from the sleeve of my leather jacket,
the old one with a patina of late nights and louche company,
I glanced down the lane beyond the Alfa, and through the flurries

saw a hawthorn and holly hedge, and above it the line of a roof.
Nothing more: just the impression of ochre ridge tiles over shingles,
running to a mellow chimney. Only that, but I stopped breathing,

like at the birth of a child when she stops being a hypothetical obligation
and becomes quick, rooted in you, justifying the sacrifice of everything
that has gone before. I got back in my car and drove on down the lane.

Delivery

I

The contractions were really strong by then:
my fists were clenched so hard
I was grinding my nails into my palms
to stop myself shouting at him to hurry.

He took us round the car park
as if we were shopping at Tesco,
ignoring perfectly usable spaces
– we've got the radar or whatever it is –

the verges and the disabled parking,
not even chancing double yellow lines.
When I realised that we weren't
going to make it in time, I hit him

flat-handed, hard across the ear.
He changed tack then, pounded the horn,
put on the four way flashers, and thank God
had the sense to pull up right outside A&E.

II

Of course, I made sure I was around to take her to the hospital.
You have to, don't you, and they get you to prepare at the ante-natal,
checking that she always has her bag packed, all the usual stuff,
common sense really, plus there's petrol in the car, in case she's early:
stopping on the way to fill up at Tesco wouldn't go down well.

It was plain sailing on the day. She said she thought it was time
so we got her in the car, back seat so she could stretch out a bit,
and off we went. Not much traffic, and I took it nice and gently
over the speed bumps and kept under 30 so we didn't get stopped.
Had a bit of trouble finding a parking space, but no real problem.

Distinctions

He's walking in the woods with his son,
helping him distinguish oak from ash,
primrose from cowslip, pigeon from magpie,
remembering walks with his own father

and how later, playing here alone,
he learned the difference between
the man with a friendly dog
and the friendly man with sweets.

Slipping

We're the last up the moor road before they close it,
and the snow's as bad as I've known. The Beamer's wheels
spin and we slew from kerb to centre line, over it and back.
Ten miles to the hospital and the boy beside me is trusting me
to get us there in time. I lose control again – as we straighten up
I'm laughing to reassure him.

A London fairground, five years before, his mother's watching us
riding on the Whirling Dervish. Our car is pivoting and twisting,
and centrifugal force sucks his slight body under the safety bar.
My fingers are grasping the sleeve of his jacket. The ride bucks again
and as he slides further, his eyes fix on my face. And I'm laughing
so he can see everything will be alright.

T Shirts

Because he did not see her much during her teenage years
when he knew a father should be present for his daughter,
teaching her there is nothing to fear in being different
he brought her back T shirts from the countries he visited.
Always Hard Rock Café T shirts, with the name of the city –
Mandalay, Valparaíso, Kathmandu, Marrakesh, Kolkata –
and always a different colour so she built a rainbow collection.
She wore these T shirts on nights out in London, reporting back to him
on their visits to clubs and pubs: he felt he had been there with her.
She was wearing the one from Aleppo on the night bus with her girlfriend
when they were set upon by men threatened by their public display of affection.

My Mother Mistakes Her Phone for a Shoe

I don't like to bother you, Doctor, but yesterday I used my shoe
to make a telephone call. That can't be right can it?
Are folk now expected to hold footwear to their ear to talk to their brother
in Dundee? I mean, what is the world coming to?

For a start, I need to know whether I'm still able to talk privately:
what if someone is listening on a shoe nearby, can they hear what I'm saying?
Because I wouldn't want my brother's dirty linen washed in public:
he wouldn't like that, they're very straight-laced in Dundee you know.

Can you tell me, Doctor, if I can only talk to people with court shoes like mine?
Or have they made arrangements for slippers? Are boots on a different network?
And what about where they don't have shoes: how will the poor people cope?
And, Doctor, the bill – will it come from Freeman, Hardy and Willis?

Oh, my nerves are in a right old state about this shoe-phone business, Doctor.
Is there anything you can give me?

Alternative Spaces

These stairs are steeper than she remembered

narrower, more twisting, the corners elbow

sharp: below her, the childhood rooms

echoing with unfulfilled promise,

and those closed adult places

once mysteriously different

but now unsurprising.

She is old, and age

like black treacle

is holding her

breathless

breathless

breathless

on the stairs

until at last the attic

with its alternative spaces

and eyes still open to the future.

Some Things about Last Christmas I'm Sure of

They set off for home at six on Boxing Day.
It had been a busy Christmas for her.
All the family had been demanding her attention.
Once she mistook her grand-daughter's shoe
for some new kind of mobile phone.
We put that down to the macular degeneration.
Another time she couldn't get up the stairs.
We thought it was tiredness.
The call from my father came at seven the next morning.
I had the car keys in my hand when my son came downstairs.
He said, 'It's Gran isn't it'.
When I got to Milton Keynes she was unconscious.
The pneumonia did not respond to the drug of last resort.
I knelt beside her bed and told her I loved her.
I'm not sure whether she responded to my squeeze of her hand.

Loveshack

A hinged formica table top makes a teepee in his path.
A wheel, unnaturally small, tucks into the hedge.
He turns the corner, and an Alpine Sprite caravan,
almost as old as he is, leans on the stump of an axle.

Through the misted Perspex, a madness of shelves,
doors, beds and benches; the sink and cooker gone,
light fittings stripped, piping bent where it resisted,
the yellowed walls weeping beads of polystyrene.

High on the bulkhead are nine paper letters
traced, cut, pasted up, the colours faded now.
He reaches in. As he wanders on, he's pleased
this memory at least is secure and recallable at will.

My Father Mows the Lawn

The lawn's wearing your best stripes,
true from flowerbed to privet hedge.

I open my window, smell the grass,
sharp as mustard. You reach the end

of another row and shunt around.
The motor thrums, rising as you

lengthen your stride: I close my eyes,
not wanting you to ever quite reach me.

When I open them, you're standing
arms akimbo, in black and white.

Seedling

For Mila May Neave

Late in the evening, deep in the Blackdown woodlands
where foxgloves stand like purple torches along my path
I slip, and falling see an acorn seedling no bigger than my hand
still bearing fragments of the dried leaves and pine needles
it had to push through to reach the daylight.
Daylight, whose variations and regularities
must still be as unknowable to that seedling
as the meaning of the squeaks of fledglings in the beech tree
or the play of the wind or the smoky taste of rain
or the unreliable companionship of the bracken with its busy fronds,
here today but gone tomorrow, or the nearness of full grown oaks,
solid, long-lived and understanding these things.
And I think of the impossibly small hand of my new grand-daughter
who has yet to make any sense of her world, and of how
she will grow tall and strong, learn all there is to know, and outlast me.

Acknowledgements

Poems in this collection or earlier versions of them have previously appeared in *Ambit, CISI Review, Iota, The Interpreter's House, Leighton Buzzard Observer, Magma, Rialto, Smiths Knoll, South* and *The North*.